The Zeal of Thine House has Eaten Me Up!

To the Church of the Living GOD with Love

C.E. Burns Jr.

WestBow
P R E S S
A DIVISION OF THOMAS NELSON

WestBow Press books may be ordered through booksellers or by contacting:

WestBow Press
A Division of Thomas Nelson
1663 Liberty Drive
Bloomington, IN 47403
www.westbowpress.com
1-(866) 928-1240

Because of the dynamic nature of the Internet, any Web addresses or links contained in this book may have changed since publication and may no longer be valid. The views expressed in this work are solely those of the author and do not necessarily reflect the views of the publisher, and the publisher hereby disclaims any responsibility for them.

ISBN: 978-1-4497-0508-4 (sc)
ISBN: 978-1-4497-0582-4 (e)

Library of Congress Control Number: 2010935763

All Scripture references are taken from the Holy Bible,
King James and New King James Versions.

To contact the author regarding this book or to arrange for him to speak to your men's group, go to: http://zeal-book.com/contactus.html

.

Printed in the United States of America

WestBow Press rev. date: 10/4/2010

For zeal for Your house has eaten me up, and the reproaches and insults of those who reproach and insult You have fallen upon me.

—Psalm 69:9 (The Amplified Bible)

Acknowledgments

First, I hail the Almighty, the Progenitor of all existence seen and unseen, who is the source of all inspiration and the reason all things persist.

Now for everybody else: I thank God for those close as well as those at my extended reach. I thank God for those who were distractions as well as those who helped me remain focused. I thank God for those who attempted harm upon me which, according to God's grace, deepened my strength and character with every failed attempt to deliver me to despair.

Oh, you didn't see your name, only references to Jesus? Well, I thanked Him for you, and with that I hope you'll agree that it's not about us but Him.

What shall I do if He does not answer, or how shall I go without His direction? For yet it is not Him but I who is far away. Now have I been drawn away from Him by him who hateth my soul. For he who hates my soul has won favor with that part which was crucified. But now let us journey on, for morning is near. But, if that part will not come forth with me, shall a battle be marked and set in array, and then shall death be the plot and mercy chased away? Then shall the sword not be put away nor the trumpet of war held back. Then shall unrighteousness weep and wallow in this fury which the Lord has ordained. And then will the righteous proclaim "who shall divide asunder us from the love of our God?" May the righteous say so! So shall they lay in his bosom and he will embrace them, and so shall the spoiler be spoiled for their soul did love the Lord. (Pause and reflect!)

In fasting did I find Him and He was ever so bright. How fair, how beautiful is He there is none to compare. Foolish men hold cheap glass toward the heavens and say, "Ah, how great this thing that I have." But the wise knoweth the diamond that is marked above all of these. And so is the Lord the foundation of the wise and the hope of the prudent. And this do His children know. (Pause and reflect!)

Introduction

THANK YOU FOR TAKING THE TIME to peruse the pages of this book. God inspired me to write it to confront a crooked ideology concerning the governing of the church (in particular in the United States). By all that is illustrated, we can conclude the church is asleep! I understand that you, as a reader, especially you who are active in various ministries, are asking, "Where does he come from with that?"

Some individual ministries are experiencing some success, but there is mediocrity in the body as a whole. Perhaps a noted and ranking clergy would not be as effective making such a statement because the reader would likely assume arrogance on their part. But coming from somewhat of a different arena I think that, not being any more true coming from one of lowly estate , readers will be more comfortable and less intimidated to relate.

Thank you for accepting my invitation to explore His house and to learn how the zeal for His house can consume us. Enjoy.

CHAPTER ONE:

IN THE BEGINNING

THE GOSPEL ACCORDING TO JOHN TELLS us, "In the beginning was the Word, the Word was with God, and the Word was God" (John 1:1; KJV).

Bible scholars know that the Old Testament starts with the same that before anything there was God. It was no different with the church; on the day of Pentecost all eyes (in one place with one accord) were on God. But just as with everything else man gets his hands on, the church started out in a marvelous state, and now we can only wonder at what it's been reduced to.

In the Old Testament, God talks to man in the Garden. By the time we get to the book of Malachi, man is being set up for a several-hundred-year silence from God because of man's sinful state. In the New Testament, we see all eyes fixed on the Lamb of God as John introduces our Savior. In the book of Revelation, we see the kings of the Earth (in the church he made us kings and priests) battling against Him, not wanting to lose their personal influence over the Lord's inheritance. (Rev. 1:6 KJV)

In the beginning men fasted, prayed, and sought God for revelation by the masses (for those who were believers, at least). Today, men desire to find their nuggets of faith in books (like this one) and in the media. Now,

1

I'm not trying to discourage you from reading, of course; it would defeat the purpose of my writing. But what I am trying to do is provoke you to think. I hope that you view this and any commentary about the Bible and spirituality the same way, with an open mind.

This book should make you seek God, not try to know Him. You should only seek to *know* Him through prayer, His word, and your experiences with Him. There are patriarchs, even of late church history, who get higher marks for their faith than where we are today as believers, which is to say that as time goes on and arrives at us, the condition has and is worsening.

Martin Luther sought something more in line with the divine doctrine. William Seymour sought the essence of the presence of God. G. T. Haywood sought exact clarity, and there have even been those who stated their faith through miraculous manifestations, such as Mildred Boyd. Some of these people you may not have heard of, but the point that I hope to drive home is that today there is more man and less God in the church, leaving the church in a condition of illustrating only superficial proofs of faith.

Most churches fall under the category of "having a form of godliness but denying the power thereof" (2 Tim. 3:5; KJV). We come together on certain designated days and share songs and experiences, we listen to a refined dissertation of commentary on the Scriptures, and then we shake hands and go home. Many would ask, "What do you have a problem with there?" and I would answer that there is no supernatural evidence that God is in the room nor does the evidence rank abundant in reports of lives being lived as spiritually regenerated! And you say, "But people expressed joy in the dance and came to the altar with tears, and there is such growth in the ministry that God must be in it."

I challenge you with this: those people who danced and cried have they experienced any significant change outside of church? Are those people winning people? And the people who they win do they bear fruit as well? We all agree, I'm sure, that if something isn't growing, then it is dying or dead. But let me take you a step further to say that just because something is growing doesn't mean it's on the right track.

People mistake a growing ministry for being the will of God. I know this sounds cynical, but I bring you a radical quote, "The zeal of thine house has eaten me up" (Pss. 69:9; KJV)

We have to change the way we think success works if we want biblical success (results). At the beginning of the church, dancing in the aisles was not the criterion that determined whether God was present or if there was excitement. In the beginning, they looked for the "power thereof" to be manifested in the church.

Paul wrote to the Corinthians in his first letter, "And I, brethren, when I came to you, came not with excellency of speech or of wisdom, declaring unto you the testimony of God" (1 Cor. 2:1; KJV). How did he come to them? Well, in the beginning, after the preaching there was proof to back up what they had just finished talking about. In the beginning, they had what Jesus said a believer would have: "Signs shall follow them that believe" (Mark 16:17; KJV).

He was not talking about a social behavior pattern; on the contrary, He meant a supernatural display being manifested somewhere in the believer's life. If we as believers are to resemble what the early church believed in, we must first raise our expectation beyond what all of us have allowed. Oops! Yes, I said it, *allowed.*

As a country, we can't afford not to have tolerance for variation and people who are different. This I embrace. But perhaps it is divinely sanctioned, for there to be a separation of church and state. It seems the church continues to cling to the government, wanting to be like it toting eager pens to make amendments as it were to the very scrolls written by Apostles in order to make allowances for social deviants in the Body of Christ. Whereas, the government should embrace all things about all people (except for criminal activity) the church should not be infiltrated with things that would water down the intent of the word of God. We as the church should stand apart from the world. Many use the expression "none of us is perfect," and that's true, but we should work toward perfection (see 2 Cor. 13:9; KJV).

Taking you, the reader, into the next phase of our focus, I submit to you that anything successful in its beginning must maintain the same principles that brought it success. Let's take a corporation, for example. The principles a corporation are governed by should be in its mission statement. If the corporation derails from the concepts of its mission statement, it should be because the mission or purpose has changed—and it should hopefully change for the better, although this is not always the case.

The Church's mission cannot be changed; it has been expressed in the word of God from its beginning to its transition. Jesus expressed the Church's mission when He read it before those who listened in the synagogue. He said, "The Spirit of the Lord is upon me, because He hath anointed me to preach the gospel to the poor; He hath sent me to heal the brokenhearted, to preach deliverance to the captives, and recovering of sight to the blind, to set at liberty them that are bruised, to preach the acceptable year of the Lord" (Luke 4:18–19; KJV).

Since this mission has not changed for the eternal church (those who are written in the Lambs Book of Life who will be raptured Rev. 21:27 KJV) why has much of the visible church, in most cases and many respects, left from its first love of being an acceptable sacrifice and testimony?

Let's go back to the example of the corporation, which should be easier to understand. When a corporation fails, whose fault is it overall? Is it the fault of the workers? It shouldn't be, because if the workforce refuses to be directed, it is up to management to correct that problem, sometimes resulting in termination. I believe that the success of any entity depends on its head, which is everything's beginning.

Chapter Two:

Power in the Head

For everything, except for God Himself, there is a beginning. And for everything that is, there is a central command post. There's nothing concerning the human body that can truly be said to have a mind of its own. If there is a problem with something not functioning the way it should, it's usually due to a neurological disorder. But even if it is for some other reason, it never is because a hand grew a brain. If the brain is damaged, then the whole body will suffer as a result. But if a limb is damaged, it does not (except in cases of extreme trauma) disable the brain from functioning.

I can lose a toe, but unless I bleed to death from it, I can continue. But if I am shot in the head and lose all brain function, then I am done. Everything in the Kingdom of God is mapped out, having respect to a chain of command. The chain of command in God's kingdom is under the auspices of the "head."

When the head is not in its place, then the body cannot function as it should. It is said by many that we are living in the Laodicean Church age where Jesus is found outside the church doors knocking to be welcomed in. This is the dispensation when Christ is not being embraced in his own church and therefore is not being respected as the head of it. So then that would be to say that the church has been hijacked!

Then the question is, "By whom?" We want to entertain all the comfortable choices and abstain from saying something that's not popular. I would propose that leadership commenced the hijacking in wavering from the blueprint. I have heard some ridiculous reasons why the church is where it is and not as the Bible says it should be. One preacher, as I witnessed, stood in a pulpit and said, "The reason that a preacher or pastor is corrupt is because the people are corrupt." As I heard that, I cringed in my seat. Being an associate minister and not a pastor, I held my disgust within. I couldn't believe that this man was a pastor, one who should know such scripture as, "It is like the precious ointment that ran down upon the beard, even Aaron's beard" (Pss. 133:2; KJV).

I'll stop there and submit to you that the anointing that we as the church hold dear, as we ought, flows from the top down. If a people attempt to weary a good man, I would agree that it should be possible to weary him indeed. But I would disagree that people can take a good man and corrupt him. It is what comes out of a man that corrupts him, not what goes in (see Luke 6:45 KJV).

We as humans sometimes overrate ourselves, saying that we're better when we are still actually quite primitive in our ways. We all have looked at someone and said, "I would never do that." Those who are wise usually learn a life's lesson in their subsequent experience: never say "never."

In many ways, we are still wrestling with many of the same things that the first man and woman did. Adam's biggest failure, perhaps, was not in his initial fault (eating the fruit), but in his refusing to accept responsibility for his actions.

Today, this is the reason we have a court system. If every time someone did something where they wronged someone else and would own up to it, why would we have a trial to establish innocence or guilt? We need a judicial system because men refuse to judge themselves. And in the case of that preacher, who was also a pastor, he was speaking from an obvious condition of *denial*. That was not the saddest part of it all; worse was that at least eight other pastors listened on and gave their consent to his statement. That told me, as I sat horrified, of the paradigm of these men that watched and stood as under-shepherds for God's flock.

Right now you may need to pause and take a breath. Breathe, breathe, and relax. I know that many people's theology is being picked at with the implication of what I just said. Yes, I just implied that the state of the church is contingent upon those who are made leaders and also that many of the leaders (not all) refuse to view themselves as accountable. To help you cool down, let me go back to the example of the corporation. Who gets the credit when the company does well? The CEO! That's why they pay him the major bucks — because he brings success to the company, he produces positive results. If that same company fails, then it is no different—the same person is to be held accountable.

Many times those on executive levels shift the blame to those beneath them. But if those beneath the executives are not doing as they should, it is up to those in charge to find a way to get them to do it or find those who will accomplish what is needed. Why is that something that most of us will easily agree with as far as corporations go, but not accept the same concept when dealing with the church? Someone reading right now is saying, "But the church is not a company," and they're right. I use the example of the company because it involves directing the masses.

The church is not a company. It is an organism. But a company, family, a church all have this in common: the need for a leader or a head. If the head refuses to hold itself accountable, then how does it have power? It is an oxymoron to say, "I am the leader but not to blame." To be "in charge" is by definition to be accountable.

So then, it is not good enough for a pastor to say that "God is going to hold me accountable" (Heb. 13:7) when he wants his parishioners to submit themselves to him or her as they should. It is to be understood that true power comes when the head is in line with the Head; then it can flow down. There is only power in the pews when there is power in the head.

CHAPTER THREE:

THE FALLING AWAY

IN PAUL'S SECOND LETTER TO THE Thessalonians, 2:3, he informed them that there would be a falling away of the believers. We see in society in general that as we advance in every other area of our existence, we are at a decline pertaining to the issue of what is moral.

Of course, things are better than in the Middle Ages and the times of great conquerors. They're better than in the days of gangsters and the times of slavery. But I suggest that to be truly moral, one must be godly. We live in an age when even the question of what is moral is argued about. Many suggest that when dealing with what is moral, each man should decide for himself.

But then what if a man says he should not be judged if he wants to have a physical relationship with an animal? Do we say that what he does is okay as long as he believes in his heart that it is pure?

Our society says one thing, but when challenged with hard topics, it contradicts itself. There are pedophiles who feel that they are truly expressing love when they molest children. There are rapists who believe that women really wished for the crime that was perpetrated against them. We try and fool ourselves to believe that life is one big free-for-all and that whatever we decide to do should be okay. But while we may have more civil rights and less violence than in the days of the Middle Ages, we have also been falling away from the fear of God.

Yes, many have perverted the concept of who God is by saying the mayhem they were committing was for God; but in spite of all the evil that man has and will imagine, God still rules. When some in the church world question if God has a problem with homosexuality or if God has a problem with abortion, it is ludicrous.

Even though we are in the world, we are not to be of the world (see John 15:19).

The moral standard is God. When problems hit close to home, then we begin to question, "Who determines what God really means?" When our son or daughter is involved in homosexuality, it challenges everything we embraced of what or who we proclaimed God to be. When our loved one dies, then it's not necessary for one to be truly born again to be in His Kingdom. You see, we are fickle humans, wishy-washy.

"Let God be true and every man a liar" (Rom. 3:4).

So, what has prompted the body (the church) to be so comfortable with romanticizing gray areas concerning interpreting the Lord's word? How has it gotten to the point that we are even discussing whether gay priests are acceptable or not and preachers of the word of God not challenging the things that God has expressed discontent over?

There was a young man named Saul in the Bible tending to his father's asses. This young man was taken captive by the people of God to be their king. They already had a king who is and was the King of kings, but they were doing this to resemble the world (see 1 Sam. 9). Is it not the same for us (the church)?

We ache over being different from the world, so to avoid the awkwardness of being eccentric, we find solace in being like the world. This is what Jonah did by running from his calling and what Peter did that led him to deny Christ. Now, let us go back to Saul: Saul had his greatest failure when he was commissioned by God to destroy the enemies of the people of God, the Amalekites, by performing a partial obedience. Saul's excuse for this was that he was compelled by the people—social pressure (see 1 Sam. 15:15).

See, it seems we have this thing in the church that says if we have the appearance of doing God's will, then it will be acceptable (partial obedience). Truly, though, there is no such thing as partial obedience; you are either obeying God or disobeying Him.

The church's not wanting to hurt the feelings of non-church people by being different from them has resulted in infidelity. Is it the sole responsibility of the leader (or should I say the leaders across the board in the body of Christ) to prevent this? *Yes*!

We are all accountable for our individual souls, no doubt, but the ship is the responsibility of the captain and the captain must lead the crew to secure a safe voyage. The person in charge, no doubt, does lead. But it is not always giving an example of leadership that leaders have in mind while living. If a policeman disregards the law and runs lights and speeds down the street for no apparent reason that sets an example for others. It is not the policeman's intention that others should take his action as an example to do likewise, but that's what happens. No, it is his intention that people do what they know is right. But it is the policeman's duty to uphold the law. As well, it is the public's expectation of him to personify law and order.

Celebrities constantly say that they are not role models, while they cry for your support of their next project. They solicit you and stand before you, seeking to influence you with their art. There are those who stand before people not bearing in mind that they will influence people. Songwriters who write of violence say it's not their fault that teenagers are killing like their songs depict. So, if those in spotlights say they do not influence their generations, why do they think it's so important that *their* music gets out? If it's not going to impact anything, then why bother?

Could it be that pastors (again, let me emphasize those leaders who are challenged in the area of bearing fruit) are victims of this whole scheme? Could it be that there are real men and women of God and no real saints?

If there are no real saints that would explain why people aren't listening— because there are then no sheep, and we know that only His sheep hear

His voice. That would make sense: there is a falling away because there are no more sheep. But wouldn't that also be the responsibility of the leaders? Would it be that there is no man of God because there is no church? Or is it that it would not be a church if there was no man of God? (See Gen. 2:5.)

The first man of God needed, of course, would be Christ, to die on the cross to establish a "right to the tree of life." "He that hath an ear, let him hear what the Spirit saith unto the churches; To him that overcometh will I give to eat of the tree of life, which is in the midst of the paradise of God" (Rev. 2:7).-

Since that time, where did crucial leadership fall away first?

CHAPTER FOUR:

POWER! POWER!

BY NOW SOMEONE READING THIS IS saying, "You're playing the blame game." It's not a blame game per se, but rather a look into a problematic situation to try and determine a solution.

I'm sure we'd all agree that the church that we mostly see today and the church expressed in the New Testament scripture (namely the book of Acts) scarcely resemble each other. So then, we do have a problem to solve. Time seems to repeat itself in cycles. It seems that many events that we read about in the prophecy of the Bible have had mirror images in times beyond what they originally dealt with. This is usually where a preacher would take creative license and parallel a time from the past with something going on in the present time.

One parallel I'd like to entertain is found in the book of Ezekiel 34:8. Here the Lord is speaking to His prophet to prophesy against the selfish spirit of the men of God. In this day there is more focus put on getting material gain than is put on godliness. *Albert Einstein once asked "can one imagine Gandhi or Jesus strapped with the bags of Carnegie?"*

Is the growth of a ministry measured in bleeding money from a few dozen people, or is it measured by growing the numbers of how many people are in the ministry? Should it be our focus to tell people to stop talking about the sweet by-and-by, encouraging them to deal a little more with getting in the here and now?

And if anyone thinks the latter is an important focus, I would ask, "Do you believe time is winding up?" If you say yes to that, then why is it important to get abundance here unless your plan is to leave something substantial for the poor soul who doesn't make it in?

The church world has become all too materialistic. Our offering time has become like a lottery having a ten-dollar line, a fifty-dollar line, and a hundred-dollar line. Preachers make such statements as, "You better get in on this; you don't want to miss your blessing." So even after I gave what I believe God put on my heart to give, if I don't give the amount you're asking, my blessing will be locked in an account?

I don't mind giving at all; anyone who knows me would consider me quite liberal in my giving. I believe that the person of God (whether a male or female pastor) should not look homely, not by any measure. But if the blessings are only going up and not coming back down, then there is a problem in the flow.

When the windows of heaven are only opening on the one at the top, then there is a problem in focus. This usually means that such a leader is probably focused on the mirror image of himself.

Many pastors who teach tithing with a passion don't tithe up! It's fine for a pastor to be a financial blessing to his own ministry; however, he must also tithe up to his or her mentor (covering /*their overseer*) or whoever he or she receives counsel from (or whatever the chain of command is in their organization).

When leaders do not tithe up in fear of what they might lose, they weaken the flow of the blessing coming back down, thus supporting the spirit of poverty in the people who are following them.

Adding to the money matters, there is inappropriate management of God's people, where some act as lords over God's flock, disregarding the warning in scripture at 1 Peter 5:3.

How sad, and what a waste of spiritual resources. People, for the most part, come out of the world (as we believe it is when one is born again) looking for something different than what they had when they were in the world. People come to the church looking for peace, and many times they are finding more confusion than they dealt with before getting saved.

There are four things in the church that pervert the scenery of what a church should actually look like—the quest for *power*, jockeying for position (*politics*), exploitation of God's people (*pimps*), and the sharecropper's mentality that spreads thick throughout many areas in our church world (*prostitutes*).

The greed for power has always been one weakness that mankind has fallen prey to. In the Garden of Eden, it was power that Satan used to tempt Eve, telling her, "For God doth know that in the day ye eat thereof, then your eyes shall be opened, and ye shall be as gods, knowing good and evil" (Gen. 3:5).

It was the fear of losing power that caused Saul to seek after David's life even if it was God's will that he was fighting against (1 Sam. 18:11).

Herod the King sought the death of our Savior, again in order to preserve his status in spite of God's will (see Matt. 2:3).

Power, as we see in history even beyond the Bible examples, has been the most dangerous corruptor in the hearts of men. Along with the many pre-church age examples, today the quest for power has outweighed men's search for God's true treasurers in spiritual power.

I myself, as one who newly came born again into the church, have experienced being hunted on different fronts ranging from character assassination and interference with opportunity to even a subtle physical assault.

Many individuals are manning the helm in the church with feelings of insecurity about their positions. But this is an indictment against them for their faithlessness; if God called a man or woman to lead His flock and if that person knew the word of God, why would they fear?

When David was challenged by his own son Absalom, we saw a man who was sure enough about the promises of God that he left what God had given him, believing that if God gave it, then God would bring it back again (see 2 Sam. 15:14).

It doesn't require a lot of depth to come to the simple reason as to why this insecurity is so prevalent: people who are nervous about the security of their position have never received affirmation that the position was theirs to begin with. Those that hack at anyone who would seem to be an up-and-coming son in the church are the same ones who probably never heard from God that they were called in the first place.

The only other logical explanation is that perhaps God called these individuals, and somewhere along the way they lost faith due to the lust in their hearts. Whatever the case, the body suffers tremendously when those that should nurture are off on a hunt to feel secure about being in charge, the item of them being in charge being quintessentially evident by reason of their title and role.

Chapter Five:

Politicians

Positions of authority are not a bad thing; they are necessary. In the book of First Corinthians, Paul tells that church to let all things be done in decency and in order (see 1 Cor. 14:40).

In order to establish order, there must be a rank and file of events, conduct, and people. There's no need for me to go on and on to explain why there's a need for a pastor or deacons. To me that is as obvious as when you walk into the church and find no singing; it would feel like something is missing.

But beyond the pastor, there is another rank and file system, a hierarchy of positions that are necessary for the church. From a Biblical perspective, the names are organized differently; the office of bishop is not a higher rank of pastor but is the blanket title given to a shepherd (see 1 Tim. 3:1).

But I am not set on debating the label that we put on one position as opposed to another position; here, we would like to focus on the lack of spirituality in attaining positions. As we stated, there is a need for positions even beyond the individual local church. First, it is written in the New Testament (Eph. 4:11,12) that having a rank in leadership is for the edifying of the body and for the perfecting of the saints. Second, which may not be second at all but included in the first, there is a need for checks and balances for whatever man gets his hands in (see Deut. 19:15).

Now that we've established our need as a church for this system of positions, let's look at where it is problematic. Are you ready? Simply put, *politics* is the poison in the church by way of men salivating and scaling the hallways of their organizations for *position*!

The positions mentioned in Ephesians have nothing to do with a vote; because this is not understood naturally is perhaps one reason why certain ones (for example, prophets and apostles) are not acknowledged in many circles.

We have rankings of elders (pastors) and rankings of bishops (overseers over pastors) that make the system more anthropomorphically friendly. With this system now in place and with years of denouncing prophets, the only factor in place in choosing a leader is the people. As we move with a word (dubiously received in the message of the candidate's friend) from the Lord to the ballot box, we have repeated the history relating to King Saul. As for Saul, "he was higher than any of the people from his shoulders and upward" (1 Sam. 10:23).

Many reading right now, some pastors themselves, are saying that the powers that be are chosen of the Lord (see Rom. 13:1).

It's true that God put Saul in place to give the people what they thought they wanted, a king like the other nations. It wasn't purity that they wanted; it was someone to impress them upon sight. Today it is no different; it's the well-spoken, fluid-flowing text-digger that we chase after. And since the people demand nothing more, that leaves the field wide open for those ready to campaign instead of those who are ready for spiritual warfare.

So, instead of men who call things that are not as though they were (Rom. 4:17), we have many who simply call things that never manifest and blame it on your faith. Many of the things that we are so bold to bring to the prayer line are ridiculous and superficial, such as an itchy throat or a headache you got an hour ago that's not killing you but just isn't convenient.

All this we give fanfare to while the crippled and blind have been sold into the thinking that "God wants me blind so that He can show that even a blind man can praise Him."

Anytime in the earthly walk of Jesus, when a blind man praised Him, that person was given their sight. In order to move back to positive spiritual manifestation in the church, we have to move back to a positive spiritual method of choosing our leadership. It seems like I'm directing this at the body more than at the leaders, doesn't it? That's because the only thing that has stood before the people is what the people have allowed and put up with.

I am not saying we should have a national mutiny, but if His people who are called by His name would humble themselves, pray, and turn from their wicked ways when choosing a leader they all would evidently hear from Heaven with their fruit bearing in their choice.

This is, almost, where the preacher mentioned earlier is somewhat in the neighborhood. I still say that an evil people don't make a good man evil; but a people with mediocre goals spiritually will choose a mediocre leader when the office is open for filling.

We're not finished, though, with politics; we've only touched on when the pastoral office becomes vacant. What about when there isn't any office open, as in a local church, but rather it's merely a title spot to be filled? I've seen men send others out to speak on their behalf.

And worse, there are those who have gone so low as to pay great amounts of money as special offerings to gain favor to receive greater titles—for example, elder to district elder and district elder to suffragan bishop (which is an assistant to the bishop).

Woe unto us, who have cheered on those who have paid thousands of dollars to lead the people of God. Woe unto us, who have encouraged these men to continue in their prayer-less journey to sure destruction.

They rule out of a lust for control and advise their congregation out of the common sayings of the day's "old-school concepts." They are reluctant to heed sound doctrine because it would demand that first they step up from their spiritual lethargy.

Show me the politician who's concerned with doing right, and I'll show you someone that is not holding (and probably will not hold) the office of their ultimate desire. A politician's job is to represent the desires and the needs of the people; the man of God's job is to represent the will and desire of the Lord God Almighty.

In the world, politicians are necessary; even the Bible recognizes world systems for the world and teaches that we in the church should respect those systems, as we stated before (see Rom. 13). But putting the world system in the church is like putting new wine in old bottles (Matt. 9:17) or trying to teach sheep to be goats. The political reign must end, and the church must prayerfully seek to bring back or welcome the prophets and the apostles into the fold again.

Chapter Six:

Pimps

Prancing about in their new clothes and big rings, pulling up in their overly extravagant automobiles with haughty expressions on their faces to boot, are the *pimps*. Who is the coolest, or who is the most hard-core? Who is known for putting their foot on your throat if you get out of line? Does this sound like descriptions that would put you in mind of the "man of God?"

I am no prude when it comes to a pastor dressing well. I have no dispute with a pastor driving a car that is better than mine. Neither do I think that a pastor should walk around acting goofy and not paying attention to his posture. But let's be honest, there are some things that we see in apparel that clearly take the focus off of the service and put it on what one is wearing. I know this is a battle that goes on throughout the congregation in many churches.

But when it comes to the leader, one should not look like the quintessence of one who lusts after filthy lucre (see 1 Tim. 3:3).

Again, I'm no prude. I like hats and fine dress wear; but when it takes the focus of the people, then it needs to be toned down. I'm still talking about leaders. Let's use common sense, people; we know what a pimp looks like, for the most part, if we saw one on the street. So why act as though, because we put pimp clothes on men of God that the world looks at that person any differently than pimps in the world? They don't!

Cars that are overly dressed as well, with twenty-two-inch rims—*what*! Pastors, it's simple: take a ride through the "hood." If you don't stand out apart from your surroundings, then you probably look like a *pimp*.

Beautiful robes and five-hundred-dollar to one-thousand-dollar suits, I'm with that, but "let your moderation be made known to all men, the LORD is at hand" (Phil. 4:5).

That's the less threatening side of pimping that goes on in the church. With the attire, there comes an attitude that says "serve me." In the world, the pimp is a so-called symbol of protection. If those who work for him are never in trouble, then he just sits back and collects that which he didn't work for. He appears to be doing a job; but if there is no trouble, he's only a middleman eating up resources. In order to maintain his appearance of usefulness, he must present himself as a god, even someone to be worshipped. Even when he or she preaches, they only refer to themselves when proclaiming what good things God has wrought.

So the people are as those who eagerly sit under a table waiting for crumbs to fall to the floor that they may join in on the goodness of a meal. A friend and I once did some work at a church; and after we were done, I sat outside in front of the church in his vehicle.

While we sat there, a man came up to the door of the vehicle. He seemed to be a decent person, although quite young, maybe late twenties. He asked, "Whose car is this here?" Being slightly thrown off by his tone, I answered, "We're the guys who remove your snow, and my partner is inside squaring away the payment for our service." He replied, "This here is my parking spot; I'm the pastor, so you need to move."

When my partner came out, I began to tell him of the young pastor's attitude. I further proceeded to comment to him, "What if I were just some guy who maybe had been considering visiting that church? What that pastor displayed in having no tact would've sealed the deal of canceling my plans."

After the young pastor had left my window (before my partner came out for me to share this with him), I jumped in the driver's seat and moved the vehicle myself. Once the pastor parked his car, a Cadillac but not that nice, he stepped out of the car, taking an unusual amount of time to get himself situated. He had on a sporty-looking mink jacket with a pullover hood and carried a briefcase with a shoulder strap.

As he walked, the shoulder strap kept slipping off of his shoulder due to the bulkiness of the jacket. But instead of using the handle, as the briefcase also had the traditional handle as well, he wrestled with the strap all the way to the door, which was about seventy-five feet from his car. I'm thinking while watching this, "Yep, all this matches the attitude that he just showed me." In order for him to maintain a certain style, he'd rather fight to keep the strap on his shoulder than look common and put the briefcase in his hand.

So it didn't surprise me when thirty seconds later, a red car pulled around the corner into the church parking lot. A man with a cigarette in his mouth walked from the car to the church. He threw down his cigarette and then walked into the church while lip-synching hello to me. Now, I know no one is perfect; yes, I know there are some people who, although they're in the church, may still have issues.

But I thought, "Couldn't he have smoked at home?" But then I thought, "I guess with his pastor being so openly belligerent, what he's doing wouldn't strike him as awkward." My partner came out and told me some equally bewildering things about his experience inside, as well as what happened on the other side of the door after the pastor labored his way in with his shoulder-strapped briefcase. In all of this, obviously no one asked, "What would Jesus do?"

After leaving that scene, I didn't feel that I had left a place of refuge, but rather a compound of some sort. Self-centeredness, disregard, and alienation were the impressions I was left with after leaving that church.

Of course, this is an extreme case but not a rare case. There are many men and women who in various ways are more worried about who's respecting them than they are worried about whose life is being translated from broken to marvelous. So many are stuck on lavish appearance and avoid concern for God's righteousness.

As you can see, the clothes that a man wears say a lot about what kind of man he is (search this sentence, and you may find metaphors more than literal meaning). In the world, something else characteristic in a pimp: pimps usually are not comfortable when other men are in close proximity to them. Pimps are usually surrounded by women. To them, women are not a threat to their program but the fuel to their program.

If ever a strong man were around, he would surely seem to be a threat. The only way the pimp would allow any man to hang around is that this man worked for him. Ever notice how so many women are in the church and men seem scarce? Ever been to a church where the women open the service, conduct the praise and worship, receive the offering, and are the altar workers at the pastor's invitation at the end of his message?

Some of us reading this, even while reading, won't quite feel conflicted with what was just asked. For many of us, the absence of men is a normal thing. Many have tried to justify this by saying that women are more spiritual than men—*hogwash*! In this nation men are in a state of spiritual bankruptcy in many places and regions, I'll admit. Is it, though, simply that men don't want to be right with God? Have men no hunger for the Almighty, filled only with the longing to indulge in darkness?

Come on! The pimp has figured a science that holds true that the pimps in the church have perpetuated in tradition. Women and men respond to things differently, as we all know. Women, being creative creatures, are stimulated by what they hear and yet are less analytical than men.

Men are direct and more literal, analyzing everything; whether their conclusions are right or wrong, wise or foolish, this is how they operate. So many things a woman may not judge about a person with pimp qualities, a man will pick up on and be turned off . (Read I Samuel 2:16-17)

There are cases when there are men who are excelling in ministry, and the pastor of that ministry becomes threatening. Real men know how to deal with other men. A man who beats his wife usually wouldn't fight a man. A bully would never go to combat with someone he'd consider his physical equal.

Why? Because all of these represent a characteristic called cowardice. As we dealt with earlier on with Saul hating David, there are pastors who instead of loving the flock and caring for the flock, envy and hate those who are strong in the flock (namely men) for fear they themselves will be viewed as useless.

The look, the accessories, the attitude, and the actions to secure their commodity are parallel across the board. So for those who are exasperated because of me calling some pastors pimps, why shouldn't I?

Chapter Seven:

Prostitutes

In respect to the concept "cause and effect," we now enter into the world of the *prostitute.* We have reviewed why, at least in my opinion, the church world has declined to a state of various social cliques and fundraising mediums, not to mention a haven for predators who prey on others to fulfill their lust for personal gain.

Now, what is the finale as far as the state of mind that people are left with if they continue to dwell in such environments? First, to stay in a situation that is by all accounts abusive, one must come to a state of acceptance. Without acceptance, which is by essence approval, one would not stay for long in an abusive situation.

Instead, a person in an abusive environment would shut down and become noticeably dysfunctional if they continued in such a situation but didn't conform in approval. So, in recognition of those who have accepted their plights and have stood in approval of the pimp's/politician's/powermonger's reality, I think an appropriate title is "prostitute." Hold on now—breathe, breathe!

Now count to ten. Okay, now I'm not talking about you, as preachers sometimes say, unless it's you. I'm not trying to personalize this to point my finger at any particular individual as much as I'm trying to highlight a trait or characteristic that, like a parasite, needs to be rooted out of the churches of God.

In the world, we know the prostitute to be "the woman of the night," the one selling her body and ultimately her soul for the delight of others that she might enjoy some meager return in the final tally for survival.

If she has a pimp, her every desire is to please her "Daddy." Wouldn't a person like this go perfectly with the person in the last chapter? Well, in order for one to exist, there must be the other to balance the scales.

There are some things that cannot exist alone. You cannot have fire without fuel. You cannot have an argument without an opposing view. You cannot have eternal life without Jesus. See, there are some things that something else is needed before they can exist.

In the last chapter, we talked about the difference between men and women; and just as a side note, in dealing with things codependent for existence, I'd like to touch on things that men do in this world that they wouldn't do if women wouldn't tolerate it. If a drug dealer knew that if he dealt drugs, no woman would touch him with a ten-foot rusty pipe, do you think he would deal drugs?

If a man who doesn't believe in working saw that he was deemed untouchable by every female around him, do you think he would sit home not concerned about employment?

You see, in order for these dysfunctional behaviors to exist, they need something to foster them. In the church, there is a co fostering mechanism to create all that we have reviewed thus far.

The pastors who fit the parts we have highlighted facilitate their congregations into a mind state to accept such pastors' liberties beyond Biblical boundaries. The congregation, on the other hand, plays their part by way of acting as though all is well with little or no challenge.

Just like the prostitute, many have allowed their minds, hearts, and sometimes bodies to be offered up short of the altar of God, landing on the table of exploitation to be lulled into a cycle of a never-ceasing vacuum draining them of abundant life and purpose. When it is obvious that an individual is not right with God, it's okay to say we need to pray for them and not get on their case too bad.

But taking into consideration that leaders are human too, we have made too many concessions and excuses for those who should live above the average man. Wake up, layperson! It's time you have a higher expectation of the one who is supposedly there to help than you have of yourself who came broken.

Just like the woman who stays in an abusive relationship using excuses to cover her path says, "He's only human, he didn't mean it," those in the church have latched on to making excuses for those who refuse to raise the bar in their own lives. I am not talking about a leader who has one fault or a few faults; I'm talking about someone who has a condition.

A fault can be a temporary thing, whereas a condition comes about over a period of time and is lasting if not dealt with. When a leader has a condition that is not conducive to growth for those that he or she will stand before, should it be the burden of others? So much slips through the cracks and into the ears of those needing the nourishing elements of the word of God, who instead are violated with desecrated viruses that the political device of choosing leaders cannot filter out.

Why should a spiritually ill-equipped leader be given excuses? In this country, no one goes to jail for not accepting what they perceive as a spiritual calling (as it is questionable if many of these are called; and if called, even more dubious if chosen).

So, if it was their choice to step into the position of leader, then it was their responsibility to prepare themselves not only mentally (we earlier referred to these as text-diggers) but emotionally and spiritually. The preparation is ongoing and should be unrelenting. If you know nothing about working on cars, why should you think to get hired as a mechanic? If you can't count, then why should you get hired by a bank? So then, if you are not born again and spiritually mature, why do you think you are qualified to be a leader in the most significant movement in all *time*, the *church*? That one was for all of us to read.

Now then, saint of the Most High, what think ye? Is there really any excuse that you can find that is good enough for the person you'd like to make it for? One day that prostitute will come across someone who will look into her eyes and think that she's the most beautiful creature he's ever seen.

But if she does not ready her mind, when he speaks to her from his heart of the beauty that he feels for her, she will miss it, counting it as another game being thrown at her. Let us not be so caught up into the system of pimps that we do not hear the Lord's voice while he is speaking in the sanctuary of our hungry souls.

Let us not be trapped in a mindless funnel twirling stagnant and downward, never challenging anything because "nobody's perfect."

Unlike the prostitute, who has probably never known real love, we don't have an excuse where we can say we've never known anything but abuse, if we've been made to know salvation. The old ragged attitudes and compulsions going about craving temporal fixes, we can no longer hold onto as a crutch of excuses.

"If any man be in Christ, he is a new creature: old things are passed away; behold all things are become new" (2 Cor. 5:17).

Chapter Eight:

Prophets

There's not a more beautiful feeling, save the presence of the Lord, than for one to be able to perceive that there is a true prophet in the house. What a delight it is for the hungry, thirsty soul to know that what will be coming across the audio system this Sunday morning will be the untainted word of life.

Not someone that's going to spend time dabbling in mere storytelling or amusing the people with a downy voice, but someone who rightly divides the word of Truth and makes application in today's terms that one may apply it to their life. This is what the Lord was referring to, true prophets, when He said, "The laborer is worthy of his meat" (Matt. 10:10).

A true prophet is just that, a laborer; one of the translations is "toiler."

How can you not toil in the night on your knees and in the day ministering to the saints of the Most High in fear and yet in great joy and still profess to hear God as clear as a bell on a calm day? A true prophet is constantly in the process of knowing God; that means first, he keeps the word of God (see 1 John 5:3).-

As you continue in the text of 1 John, everything is tied together bringing us to an understanding that knowing and loving God require a mutual prerequisite. In human terms, we accept the concept of levels of love.

Even when we know the definition of love, we accept the words "I love you" from those who have displayed contempt for us. There are those who would genuinely like to believe that they love others, but the sad reality is that they have not known love. It is first necessary to receive love in order to give it.

A man or woman of God shows the love that they have for God in their striving. One may not be perfect at every turn, but are they noticeably striving for anything higher in the Lord? True prophets do just that—they look for God.

They reminisce on Him until He shows them something in the power of God for the now. The prophet (as opposed to the politician or pimp) chases through his life's tumult in search of the Master's whisper. It's easy for him to be caught in a daydream thinking about the goodness of the Lord and not feel that he's being "too heavenly minded."

The prophet reads the Scripture and finds the voice of God still ringing; he reads the Songs of Solomon and finds no perversions to cleanse himself of, because he's discerning spiritually. This is one who is of the sort who constantly asks that he be allowed to perceive a thing the way God meant a thing.

So then, He whose name is wonderful becomes center focus amid the day's obligations and harvesting. Now imagine such a one standing before the people of God. Imagine as this individual's mouth opens. Are you, the reader, in the room with me? The prophet's words are sure, yet bear the same skeletal properties as the words of others.

The prophet's efficaciousness is not a product of talent or of self-taught skill; nor is it from formal schooling (although I advocate formal schooling) that the prophet receives his enlightenment.

Because he is his Beloved's and his Beloved is his (Song of Sol. 6:3) it's easy for him to both speak of the Redeemer (Isa. 41:14) with authority and as well be in the place of heavenly company (Heb. 12:22/Eph. 2:6).

Prophets are those who when they pray for you, it causes you to look for what was prayed for in expectation that it's coming *now*. Never to fear people of God, even when my own life has not measured up, I stand sure on this; if I'm not up to par, I know that somewhere God has a man that has not bowed his knee to Baal (see 1 Kings 19:18).

Maybe it is where you, the reader, are that there is need for you to salvage the leader you have in prayer; and then maybe it is time to salvage your own life because that leader won't hear God. Whatever the case, know that it is the prophet being in the house that makes all the difference because the prophet came with God, so then God is with the prophet (see 1 Kings 17:10–16).

Chapter Nine:

The Pulpit

When the prophet is in the house, we can expect the correct flow in the order of the anointing. "Pulpit" means stage or platform. For too long a time, it has been the place that men have used for their own antics.

We have perverted it in such ways as to stage a circus, stage an assault on the people of God, and even stage robbery during offerings. It has been abused so much that many leaders stay out of the pulpit when they preach and teach due to the stigma that has been attached to it from preaching hit men. I contend that there is still great significance in the pulpit. As for the Body of Christ, people must be led.

The job of the prophet concerning the pulpit is to bring the focus back to the pulpit as the place to set a platform, at least initially, for Yeshua (Jesus). Just as the ointment ran down Aaron's beard (Pss. 133) eventually making it to a gathering at the hem of his robe, the same is the order from the pulpit to the pews.

When we recognize order and flow and come into alignment with those concepts, our blessings are the type that overtake us (Deut. 28:2) instead of the type that sputter like a stalling car, which, yes, still gets you to your destination.

Precious oil was never meant for just one part of the body. This is why it was poured over the head, knowing that it would run down. As long as the head is attached, then the body will also be affected by that which was poured on the head.

Note that God did not command a solid substance to be used to anoint. It has always been His intention that the whole body be anointed, not just the head. When the woman with the alabaster box came and anointed Jesus with the precious ingredients in her box, with boldness, she poured it first unto His head.

Notice that she wasn't finished; she continued her adorning of the Savior, also anointing His feet with the same ointment, her tears, and drying His feet with her hair (Luke 7:37–38).

The platform for her was the opportunity of the occasion. The Lord is always waiting to come in and drown us in His goodness. The Bible tells us in 2 Chronicles 16:9, "The eyes of the Lord run to and fro throughout the whole earth, to show Himself strong in the behalf of them whose heart is perfect toward him."

When the prophet is in the house and sets the order of the house according to the word, he has then made God a platform. Once a platform is in place, "the word's the limit."

People are not being healed because there is no platform. There is little deliverance coming to the altar because the emphasis has been taken from the place just beyond the altar where the priest must go to minister; so then, how can there be a flow to the altar if the order of the flow has been disrupted?

We have become a people looking for the new thing to cast down. We are quick to cast down traditions from when someone heard from God in, not so long ago, church history.

We are quick to cast down the concept of religion, not realizing that once you put something into a form of any sort and practice it, it then becomes a religion to you. What we mean to cast down, on that note, are religious spirits; which is doing away with "just doing things just to do them." We said we were cleaning up God's house and have gotten into throwing out things that are necessary, like the furnace, and tearing apart the foundation that the house cannot stand without.

Traditions should only be dismantled when they conflict with the word of God, period. If it goes beyond what He said, get it out. If it doesn't line up with the word, get it out (see Rev. 22:18–19).

Because we thought we could take "order" out of God's house and it would still work, God has taken order out of our house. Why is our flow disrupted? Because we disrupted His flow!

If the platform God is looking for to perform on is not replaced, He will continue to allow the metastasizing theater of man's ghastly imagination and terrestrial supernova-like surreal events that plague our existence. We don't provide Him a platform because we believe our advancements have shown us a better way, yet neither is He moving in those places that we have clinged to revealing it impossible that our new way is the genuine article.

He's left, as it were on His own, to bring the blessings that He's faithful to bring for the few that genuinely believe and pray for them through the thick cloud of unbelieving ersatz witnesses; for those attempting to create a platform in the midst of an environment that is Edging God Out He will deliver. We've asked Him to show up and show out but not provided a platform, so He makes His own and does as we have asked. He shows up and He shows out.

CHAPTER TEN:

THE PEWS

THERE IS A SYSTEM USED IN the corporate world called the "Six-S" program. It is a program that teaches companies how to run their businesses as efficiently as possible. That means the least amount of waste in time, movement, and energy in order to complete a task. Not to get too deep into the program itself, there is one saying that is used in this tactical approach (created by the Japanese): "there is a place for everything, and for everything there is a place."

People, like things, are most useful when they are where they belong. My mind goes back to a message preached by a certain pastor titled "Stay in your place." The ideology of the message was the same as the foregoing saying.

When people are not in the place that they are anointed to be in, then they disrupt the flow of the anointing of God (see Num. 2).

Let me deal with this one issue on the top, only because it's been chased

down enough even when no threat of it existed. IF YOU WERE NOT THE ONE INSTALLED AS THE PASTOR, QUIT ACTING LIKE THAT'S WHO YOU ARE. Now, can we move on?

There are many other ways that people are not positioned in the body as they should be. Some are out of position by commission of an act, and others by omission of an act. Many suffer from omission of a certain kind called *laziness.*

There are so many people in the church who think they are only supposed to come and watch. They leave home getting up from the couch to the car, sit for five or six miles, then mosey into the church to their favorite spot, and *sit.*

When they're asked to stand for the reading of the word (Neh. 8:5) they mumble (some within themselves and others quietly outwardly) and slowly move into position.

Laziness is the cancer in the church among the pews. Prophets and Prophetesses, if you have a good worker in the church, don't get him to do everything; you might work him to death. You need that one; don't kill him.

Concentrate on giving that one your important delegated duties. I touch on this for the benefit of those who are hoping to have the oil run over them as it comes down from the head.

I must put on notice those who are in the pews that whether you are in place or not, the oil *will* flow down; it's just a matter of if you will be in-line with the flow. As I mentioned in the previous chapter about how God will bring His flow regardless of disasters, the same holds true for the pews.

It behooves us to be ready for the blessing! When the prophet is in the house and sets a platform, the anointing of the Lord will surely flow. Now, if one appears to be in place but actually is not, the anointing will flow and bring damage to such individuals instead of blessings (see 2 Kings 7:17).

So whatever it is that the Lord has called you to do, get to it! Don't be the one not believing but still going through the motions (religious spirit), standing in the gate only to be trampled by the coming blessing.

Maybe the problem in many cases is that people don't know what they're supposed to do and they haven't asked. The victory that overcomes the world is our faith (1 John 5:4), but if our faith has no action it's not alive (see James 2:20).

So then, should we come to the body of Christ like a parasite only looking for what the body can do for us? Sing for us? Encourage us? Pamper us? God forbid!

"But without faith it is impossible to please him: for he that cometh to God must believe that he is, and that he is a rewarder of them that diligently SEEK HIM" (Heb. 11:6).

The pew is a standard of positioning, not measurement. It is a place and not meant to be an occupation.

The pews cannot be put ahead of the pulpit, no more than the pulpit can be put ahead of God. Only when God's condition of order is met and men stop thinking of themselves more highly than they ought to, can miracles, blessings, and healings, along with deliverances and families, be mended and backsliders come back and overall the move of God be wrought.

CHAPTER ELEVEN:

THE PARISHIONERS

THERE WAS A WOMAN THAT JESUS engaged in conversation at a well near a place called Sychar in Samaria. While in dialogue with her, the Lord mentioned to her something that God looks for: God looks for a certain type of person to be delighted in, a true worshipper, someone that worships in spirit and in truth (see John 4:23).

One definition for the word "parishioner" is "worshipper." There is nothing more beautiful to God than someone worshiping Him out of their whole heart.

I think He helps us understand His longing for worship when we sing certain worship songs and it seems that He sweeps in the room and floods our hearts with a feeling that only He has on us.

If you, the reader, have never directed words toward God from your heart filled with affection for Him and Him only, you should try now by directing your attention upward toward His throne and telling Him, "I love you." Did you feel that? I did it along with you in the sense that while I am writing these words telling you to do it, I did it myself. And you know what? I felt the flow. The worshipper is what God was after with Moses giving the law to Israel, with David getting the promise, with a virgin bearing the Savior who sacrificed Himself on a hill that we call Calvary.

A love and a yearning so deep, passionate, and compelling that this Redeemer rose from the perils of death, ascended into heaven, and is seated in the throne of power with fire for the passion in His eyes (Rev. 1:14) and for all who will receive Him. He gives the authentic quintessence of Himself to dwell within them. He did all this that He might have, on Earth, worshippers who worship in spirit and in truth.

So then, once the prophet is in the house and the platform is set and order is in the pews, and everyone is in their place according to their course, *let's worship Him who is faithful and true.*

The Bible tells us in Psalms 22:3 that God dwells or resides in our praise-He causes the evidence of His presence to swell and become detectable to the worshipper. Praise is a reaction to an action. That means God is praised because He has done something. For example, when someone amuses us, we respond with something to acknowledge that something has been done; we give applause or a pat on the back.

Worship is the positive response to the properties, characteristics, and/or value of something; it is someone giving adoration in humility as a result of recognition. We established from 1 John that if you don't know and keep the word of God, you can't love or know God. You can praise the action of a pot of gold falling from the sky into your backyard, but you can only worship the sender if you attach a source.

You can praise Him, the Lord, because someone told you the blessings came from Him; but you can only worship Him, in all honesty, if you know something of His attributes.

Going through the motions of worship but never having any connection or experience with God would be like three blind men standing before the *Mona Lisa* painting and acting as though it was the most beautiful painting ever! The only way to know that painting is to see it. Not that we can see God (John 1:18), and not that we have to, but because we experience God in our lives both in His word and Him dwelling within us, do we know Him. Not just anyone can be called a parishioner.

This, I hope, will be one of the most controversial literary works written in modern times. Not because of a great selection of words on a page, but because of what it ultimately challenges us to do—*worship*.

When the prophet worships, he has laid a platform; and then when the parishioners worship, the people first being in their order, the world is set afire and turned upside down (see Acts 17:6).

As a mighty structure would be without pillars, so is life without
dreams.
As one to live without air is as one to live without dreams.
I saw the vagabonds of this world
walking always awake.
They have neither closed their eyes
nor stole away into a blissful dreamscape.
And then there were those in castles,
that do always dream.
Their lawns were plush and their trees
do always give shade.
So then to these things I've concluded,
Wonder and Amazement beget inspiration,
Inspiration invokes dreams, and Dreams will
without fail birth Greatness.
So then dream I of the zeal of the Lord's house.

Chapter Twelve:

The Zeal of Thine House

In the second chapter of the Gospel of John, Jesus went to Jerusalem for the Passover feast. Once He arrived, He found those who had made a marketplace out of the temple. All the things that were being handled at the temple were necessary, but they were not in their proper place nor being used in equitable function. Today also we have put things where worship belongs.

It is our duty as believers to not allow the Lord's house [as in the church building as well as the house of our earthly tabernacle (2 Cor. 5:1)] to become overrun with criminal activity and/or worldliness.

This is my challenge to the church world, especially in the United States of America:, to burn in your hearts toward the Lord, whose heart also burns for you. What we read concerning Biblical events between 33 and 95 A.D. should as well be the experience that we are living.

Jesus told his disciples concerning the Gospel Age, without setting a cutoff within that time, that "he that believeth on me, the works that I do shall he do also; and greater works than these shall he do; because I go unto my Father"(John 14:12).

The miracles, healings, and resurrections that Jesus and the apostles of old wrought should be the milieu of the present-day church. We must dream bigger and bolder, fearing to be deemed by God an unbeliever (see Rev. 21:8).

The alternative is that when the enemy comes in like a flood, the Spirit of the Lord will be among some other group that's excited enough about Him being around that they get themselves in order. And we will be left to clean up our own destruction, while the blessings of the Lord are richly poured out in a place where they never had been before.

So Zion, Jeshurun, the Apple of His eye (Deut. 32:10), know that He began a work to finish it (see Phil. 1:6). He invested for a return, and the return expected is nothing less than marvelous and not short of wonderful (see Ps. 139:14).

Afterword

Whether you're a leader reading this or as one of the congregation in your church, because you're reading it you're in the land of the living. And if you are in the land of the living, God has given you the opportunity to seek Him better and stronger than where you may have come short.

I'm not trying to throw anyone away in writing these chapters, but rather I want to throw away attitudes that do not promote Biblical results. I now challenge you, not as if I have not many times thus far, to hunt within your spirit for a zeal for His house such that it will consume you so that you delight yourself in the Lord always.

For I look over the trees and over the peak of the highest mountain. I also stand next to the mountain and find how it is larger than I. And yet you, O Lord, are more than the mountain and moreover Thou art greater than many mountains! So who shall trouble me? Selah.

O Lord, let me count the ways how I love Thee; for to be idle am I at thirst, but to do your will then I am satisfied. In my supplication I long to meet you there; Oh! I am lost and lonely without your touch, and yet the earth is filled with your creation. Now let me count the ways and let not my heart hide it from me nor let my eyes deceive me. The ocean roars by reason of the wind; birds sing due to the coming of dawn. Even the antelope leap in joy at the coming of rain. So much more is my praise and does my heart rejoices and with my strength do I dance before Thee in Thy courts at the sounding of your voice, which comes from the mount in the New Jerusalem. Selah.